Art Festivals & Galleries: The Art of Selling Art

ART TODAY!

Acting: Stage & Screen

Art Festivals & Galleries:
The Art of Selling Art

Comedy & Comedians

Filmmaking & Documentaries

Music & Musicians

Painting

Performing Arts

Photography

Sculpting

Writing: Stories, Poetry, Song, & Rap

Art Festivals & Galleries: The Art of Selling Art

Z.B. Hill

Mason Crest

Mason Crest
450 Parkway Drive, Suite D
Broomall, PA 19008
www.masoncrest.com

Printed and bound in the United States of America.

First printing
9 8 7 6 5 4 3 2 1

Series ISBN: 978-1-4222-3167-8
ISBN: 978-1-4222-3169-2
ebook ISBN: 978-1-4222-8706-4

Library of Congress Cataloging-in-Publication Data

Hill, Z. B.
  Art festivals & galleries : the art of selling art / Z.B. Hill.
    pages cm. — (Art today!)
  ISBN 978-1-4222-3169-2 (hardback) — ISBN 978-1-4222-3167-8 (series) — ISBN 978-1-4222-8706-4 (ebook) 1. Art festivals—Juvenile literature. 2. Art galleries, Commercial—Juvenile literature. I. Title. II. Title: Art festivals and galleries.
  NX420.H55 2014
  708—dc23
                                    2014011826

Contents

KEY ICONS TO LOOK FOR:

 Text-Dependent Questions: These questions send the reader back to the text for more careful attention to the evidence presented there.

 Words to Understand: These words with their easy-to-understand definitions will increase the reader's understanding of the text, while building vocabulary skills.

 Series Glossary of Key Terms: This back-of-the book glossary contains terminology used throughout this series. Words found here increase the reader's ability to read and comprehend higher-level books and articles in this field.

 Research Projects: Readers are pointed toward areas of further inquiry connected to each chapter. Suggestions are provided for projects that encourage deeper research and analysis.

 Sidebars: This boxed material within the main text allows readers to build knowledge, gain insights, explore possibilities, and broaden their perspectives by weaving together additional information to provide realistic and holistic perspectives.

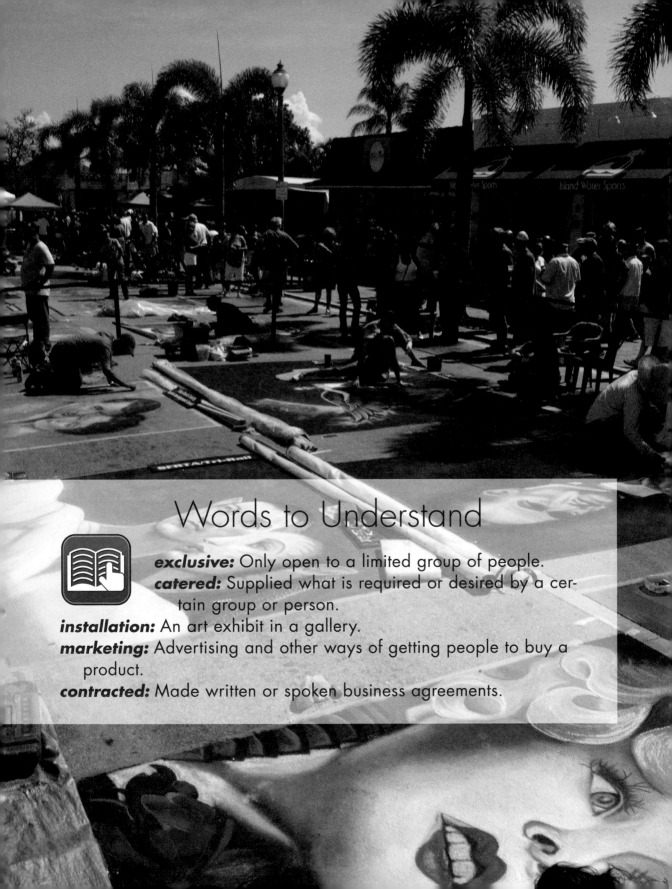

Words to Understand

exclusive: Only open to a limited group of people.
catered: Supplied what is required or desired by a certain group or person.
installation: An art exhibit in a gallery.
marketing: Advertising and other ways of getting people to buy a product.
contracted: Made written or spoken business agreements.

Chapter One

Organizing Art Festivals and Galleries

If artists simply painted, sculpted, wrote, danced, or made music in their studios, the rest of the world would never get to see it! Fortunately, a lot of art makes it out of the studio and into the world. Artists sell their art in order to support themselves and make money, but also to make sure other people get to see their art.

People who sell art may be the artists who painted or sculpted in the first place, or they may be other people whose job it is to do the selling. Art can be sold in lots of different ways—at arts festivals and fairs, in local businesses, in galleries, online, or directly from artists. Selling art is an art in and of itself. The artist or businessperson who figures out how to successfully sell art can make a comfortable living—and at the same time, make sure others get to see the wonderful art being made in studios around the world.

Art festivals are often held outdoors. This means they're usually summertime events.

ART FESTIVALS

Art festivals come in all shapes and sizes. Local high schools hold small arts-and-crafts fairs as fundraisers. Cities organize large fairs and festivals to attract tourists. Museums have art exhibits highlighting more expensive art for sale.

What all art festivals have in common is that they have art for sale, usually from many different artists. Festivals make it easy for customers to buy art, since they can browse through all the photographs, paintings, and other beautiful things. They don't need to contact individual artists and go to their personal studios—festivals bring art together in one convenient spot.

Art festivals are also fun events. In many towns and cities, they're an annual part of the spring, summer, fall, or holiday seasons and are part of the local culture. Visitors meet with their friends, eat some festival food, and take a walk around town, in addition to looking at all the art. Larger art festivals can bring tourists to cities and help local businesses get lots of customers. Some places wouldn't be the same without their art festivals.

Art festivals are often about the visual arts, but they don't have to be. The visual arts include painting, photography, sculpture, collage, pottery, prints, and film. Visual art involves objects you can touch. Non-visual art—usually referred to as performing art—on the other hand, includes dance, music, theater, and comedy. It is art you can't touch, that relies on the body and other processes to get ideas and emotions across to its viewers.

Performing arts festivals give artists chances to get together and perform dances, operas, and concerts for interested audiences. Each festival will often focus on one particular art with a particular theme. A summer folk festival, is one example, and a modern dance festival is another.

An artist can display his art at a gallery. People enjoy coming to look at it, and they also have the opportunity to buy it.

Make Connections: First Fridays

 Several cities in the United States have monthly events called First Fridays, which combine an art festival experience with art galleries. On the first Friday evening of every month, art galleries and museums open their doors and encourage the public to visit. There might be live music on the street, children's art activities at the library, and other entertainment going on at the same time. The city or a group organizing the First Friday advertises and produces information about the galleries. They might even set up a trolley or bus to take people from gallery to gallery. The First Friday idea isn't a new one—in fact, the African American business community has gathered together to network on first Fridays for many years.

ART GALLERIES

Art galleries are another type of place to show and sell art. Unlike art festivals, they're not one-time or once-a-year events—they're more permanent businesses whose purpose is to sell art.

There are many different kinds of galleries. In the past, art galleries were more **exclusive** and **catered** to very wealthy people. They weren't open to the general public; instead, they worked with wealthy art collectors to find and sell the works of art those collectors wanted. Some of these sorts of business still exist, but that's not how the majority of galleries work that are open today.

Some of today's galleries belong to one artist who uses it as a space to both create and sell his art. He wants to make a living from his art and dedicate his time to creating and selling art. Having a gallery can offer him an easier—though usually more expensive—way to really focus

These two art galleries are arranged very differently. Each has its own feel—but both display painters' works and give people a chance to buy them.

on professional art. Customers can come directly to the gallery to meet with the artist and browse through his work.

Still other galleries show the art of multiple artists, or they have rotating collections that allow customers to stop by and see new art every time they come in. These galleries may have themes, or they may highlight local artists who want to sell their art.

Some art galleries sell arts-and-crafts made by people in other countries, including handmade items like sculptures, baskets, and home décor. These sorts of galleries offer a space for artists in other countries to gain access to customers in North America who have more money to spend on art. The artists can then rely on sales from their art to make a living back in their home countries.

CURATORS

People who organize galleries are usually called curators. To curate means to design and take care of an art exhibit in a museum or gallery. Curators decide how to set up a gallery, what sort of art should go in it, and how to display it.

Curators for galleries that showcase a lot of different artists' work may decide to have a show based on a theme. Maybe a curator creates a show about living in a certain neighborhood or about technology. Then she finds artists whose work fits in with that theme and asks them if they would like to contribute. Then the curator will need to decide exactly how to display all the works of art she's getting. She may start with a floor plan and map out the gallery exhibition. Lots of techniques are used to organize art, while hanging it on the wall or placing it in the room. Gallery shows can be as simple as hanging a picture on the wall with a foot of space between each one. Or they can be complicated and involve hanging art at lots of different heights while also incorporating text written directly on the walls. Setting up the *installation* can similarly be simple or complex, depending on the display plan and the type of art being exhibited.

Displaying very large works can be particularly challenging for curators.

Make Connections: Galleries in Local Businesses

Sometimes small businesses will feature art for sale on their walls. Cafés and restaurants are the most common sorts of businesses that do this, since displaying art to the walls adds free decoration while supporting local artists by offering that art for sale. A café might have one artist's work up for display for a month or two, before rotating it out with another artist.

A curator or gallery owner will also need to advertise each show. *Marketing* and advertising is just as important as with art festivals. The goal is to make more people aware of the gallery so they'll stop in and maybe buy some art. Grand openings often involve food, entertainment, and of course art! The artists themselves are usually at openings, so they can chat with friends and potential customers about their art.

Galleries often have grand-opening receptions for new exhibits. An artist may be ready to introduce a new body of work in his personal gallery, or a rotating gallery might have a new show ready to go. In either case, advertisements will let customers know they should check the gallery out for some new art. Many galleries send out invitations. They aren't always exclusive invitations, but they're a little more personalized than a flyer.

ARTIST COOPERATIVES

Setting up a gallery can be expensive. One artist alone might not be able to afford to pay rent and utilities, not to mention advertising, for a gallery on his own. And chasing down new galleries to show work in can be exhausting and stressful.

Research Project

This chapter covers the details of one artist cooperative in Tennessee. Find another art gallery online that isn't a co-op, and research out how it runs. You can choose from the list of gallery business types listed in this chapter, or do your own investigation and find another model. Use the gallery's website to write a short report on why the gallery was started, what kind of art it shows, who owns it, who works in it, and how the artist or artists that exhibit in the gallery make money.

Some artists have come up with a solution called a cooperative. Cooperatives are businesses that are owned and run by a group of people who work together for a common purpose. They make decisions together and work cooperatively.

In the case of art galleries, cooperatives allow artists to combine their resources and create a space to display their art and make money from it. Several artists together can afford the rent for a gallery space, where one alone might not be able to. Co-ops need to find a way to make decisions, since they involve a group of people. They might decide on a voting structure in which all artists have to agree, or in which at least half must agree.

One group of artists in Germantown, Tennessee, created a co-op several years ago. There wasn't a lot of space for artists' exhibits in town, so they decided to create their own. They leased a space in a local mall for thirty days to try out their idea. They designed a logo and created a sign for their new space, so that people would know who they were.

The group of artists who owned the co-op then **contracted** with

Text-Dependent Questions

1. Name two ways artists can sell their work.
2. How is an art gallery different from an art festival?
3. What is a curator? What are some of the curator's tasks in an art gallery?
4. Why do galleries host opening receptions?
5. How are cooperatives different from traditional businesses?

other artists who wanted to sell their art in the co-op space. New artists came to a meeting to introduce themselves. Then they joined the co-op as members and paid some dues to cover monthly expenses. The co-op allowed twenty-four artists to be members and sell their art at any one time. It kept a waiting list for other artists who wanted to join.

This particular co-op had a board of five people to make all financial decisions, rather than have all twenty-four people make decisions. Besides the board, artist-owners were expected to do certain jobs to maintain the co-op, such as marketing, cleaning, event scheduling, and keeping track of the money. Some of the artists had to be always in the gallery whenever it was open, to help customers and answer questions. Everyone took turns doing the different jobs. Each month, the co-op members changed the gallery so that it would always look different and draw in customers. Artists who exhibited there had to continually provide new work. All that hard work gave dozens of artists a great space to show their art and to become more successful than they might otherwise have been!

Words to Understand

commissioned: Paid to have a custom work of art made.

revolutionized: Changed in a big way.

Chapter Two

The History of Selling Art

Art has been around for a very long time—since the time of cave people, in fact! Some of the earliest evidence of art are cave paintings found in places like South Africa, France, and Spain, dating back tens of thousands of years. Cave paintings show horses, buffalo, and human handprints. They may have been a way that prehistoric people told stories to each other.

But while the history of art is long and varied, the history of selling art is much shorter. For a long time, art was either used to decorate everyday objects like baskets and pottery, or **commissioned** by kings and religious leaders. Ordinary people didn't buy art, because it wasn't

A pope (the leader of the Catholic Church) during the sixteenth century hired an artist named Michelangelo to paint the Sistine Chapel, shown here. It was full-time job for Michelangelo that took him many years to complete.

Make Connections

Crafts and art are both objects that are decorative and have a purpose beyond simple use. A wall by itself isn't usually considered either an art or a craft, because its purpose is just to hold up a roof and to provide protection. However, if that wall is painted with decorations, its purpose is also about beauty and expression. People often regard art and craft as different things, but the line between them can get blurry. The purpose of art is generally thought of to be purely expression. A sculptor sculpts because he wants to tell a story or express an emotion or idea. Craft, on the other hand, is more useful and involves the process of work. A basket weaver creates her craft to hold food, but it may also be decorated to tell a story or express an emotion or idea.

really for sale. Instead, they made their own art that was useful (a form of art that is often referred to as "craft.")

In the past few hundred years, however, more art has been organized into exhibits, and more art is for sale. Now, many ordinary people can afford to buy art made by professional artists. Artists no longer have to depend on kings and churches to make a living. They can rely on selling art to make money and support themselves.

GATHERING ART TOGETHER

For a long time, powerful leaders collected art to show off their power. Think about the thousands of clay soldiers commissioned by the Chinese emperor Qui Shi Huang in 200 BCE and discovered in 1974. The soldiers, often called the Terracotta Army, were meant to guard the emperor in

The Terracotta Army is made up of more than 8,000 soldiers. More than 700,000 workers and artists worked together to create them.

London's National Gallery was one of the first art galleries, and it is still open today.

the afterlife. They are lifelike and very detailed. Although their paint has worn off, they were once covered with vivid colors.

In the early 1700s, a German prince named Johann Wilhelm II built the first known structure meant to hold an art collection. Before this, art had been displayed in palaces. The prince's art wasn't for sale, but it was a forerunner of the art galleries of today.

In the 1800s, art exhibitions began to become popular. Wealthy people who owned a lot of art would open up their galleries to the public, rather than keeping the art locked away. The British Institution for Promoting the Fine Arts in the United Kingdom organized some of the first loan exhibitions too. These shows gathered art from several different art collectors to create a new, temporary display. The British Institution also bought paintings for a more permanent collection. That collection eventually turned into the National Gallery in London.

A patchwork quilt like this one is usually considered to be a form of craft, since it is both beautiful to look at and useful as a bed covering.

Research Project

 Pick one kind of art and see if you can find more information on how it has been bought and sold throughout history. You can choose painting, sculpture, photography, crafts, or even a non-visual art like dancing or music. Who purchased it during earlier times? When did it become available to a wide range of people? Who buys and sells it today? Write a short report on at least three major changes in the way your chosen art has been sold.

MAKING ART MORE ACCESSIBLE

For a long time, only very wealthy politicians, religious leaders, and merchants bought art. Today, though, people with less wealth purchase art. The trend started in part in the Netherlands in the 1700s, when painting was very popular. So many painters and apprentice painters were at work that the price of paintings fell enough to allow less wealthy people to decorate their homes. Prints of paintings made it even easier and cheaper to get art.

Today, art isn't always cheap, but it is affordable for many people. It isn't reserved just for people with a lot of power (although those people can still afford a lot more art than everyone else!). Many people have a painting or two, some photography, or some small sculptures in their homes. Prints of famous art works are also popular in many places, from college dorm rooms to bank lobbies.

The line between craft and art is often blurred, and something that was once a craft can also turn into an art form. This quilt is a good example. It is not meant to be useful; it is meant only to be art.

Text-Dependent Questions

1. Who were the primary purchasers of art for most of history?
2. What role did the British Institution have in promoting public art?
3. According to the sidebar, what is the difference between arts and craft?
4. Explain how people who weren't extremely wealthy could begin to buy art.
5. How has the Internet changed the way people sell art?

SELLING ART IN THE AGE OF TECHNOLOGY

An even more recent development when it comes to selling art is the Internet. Today, artists have even more options for connecting with customers. They can create virtual galleries on websites to show off their art and make blogs to talk about it. Through the Internet, artists can connect with customers all over the world, as long as they're willing to ship their work to where their customers live.

The Internet has **revolutionized** a lot of things, including selling art. If you're looking for a particular piece of pottery, you can search online for the perfect artist. The online art market continues to grow every year, and someday more art may be sold online than in person.

All this doesn't mean that art festivals and galleries are going away any time soon, though. It's still fun to get together with other people and look at art that's not on a computer screen!

Words to Understand

grant: Money given by an organization to be used for a certain purpose.

Chapter Three

The Business
of Selling Art

In order to dedicate their lives to making art, most artists have to make money. Art festivals and galleries are two ways that artists can support themselves through art. Art gallery owners and festival organizers often make money, but the artists whose work is displayed do as well.

SELLING AT A FESTIVAL

Selling at art festivals is a little more complicated than just showing up and setting up a tent. Artists need to go through a process before they even arrive.

First, artists usually have to have a licensed business before they can sell their work. Licensing a business is a fairly simple process that

This enormous art fair is held every year in London.

involves filling out an application through the town or county where the artist works. Many states require that only artists who make a certain amount of money must be licensed, but they allow all artists to get a license. It's better to be safe than sorry, especially if an artist ends up being more successful than anticipated.

Next, artists need to find festivals at which to sell. Towns and cities around the country host thousands of festivals every year. Each one has tens, hundreds, or even thousands of artists who are all set up for sale year after year. The more established festivals don't have to reach out to artists—the artists reach out to them.

It costs money to sell at an art festival. Every person or business that wants to set up a booth has to pay a fee. The fee depends on the festival but ranges from about $50 to a few thousand dollars. Artists are willing to pay because it gives them access to paying customers.

Artists must also submit an application to the festivals of their choice. The applications usually ask the artist to submit photos of her art. Festival organizers want to make sure the quality of art is what they want at their event, and they also make sure there aren't too many artists in one medium selling. If all the artists that show up at a festival offer similar photographs, for example, no artist is going to do particularly good business.

Selling art can be hard work. Artists who sell at festivals have to be at their booths the whole day (minus a bathroom break or two). Artists who stand up and greet customers are usually more successful than ones that sit and read a book or relax. Artists sell more if they engage with the customers and answer questions. Setup and take-down also require a lot of time and energy. Early in the morning, artists unpack their tents, tables, equipment, and art and set it all up—and then at the end of the day, they take it all down again. Fragile art needs particular care while packing and unpacking it and moving it around. It's exhausting work!

Most art festivals are outside, so artists also have to deal with bad weather such as rain, cold, and intense heat. Festivals are usually held rain or shine, so artists need to prepare for less than pleasant weather.

Other art fairs can be small and informal, like this sidewalk fair.

They may use tent weights to keep their tents on the ground during windy weather, and add fabric sides to tents to keep out rain. They bring fans if it's hot.

People who are serious about selling at art shows end up traveling a lot. There might be a few shows in their immediate area where they can sell their work, but artists are able to sell a lot more if they travel to other towns as well.

PLANNING AN ART FESTIVAL

Art festivals don't just pop up out of nowhere. Someone has to organize them! Festival organizers have a lot of work to do before the big day, and they spend months getting it all together. Here are a few of the steps a festival organizer needs to consider and complete before the event actually happens.

- Get help. Organizing an entire festival alone is almost impossible, unless it's very small. Organizers work together, or they convince friends and other people to help out with the planning. Local artists, gallery owners, and museum workers might all be good sources to reach out to for help.
- Get a license. Organizers will need to make sure holding a festival is legal. Most towns and cities require large events to be licensed before they happen.
- Connect with the community. Art festivals do better if they have an artist or organization attached to them that people know about. Maybe a local museum wants to sponsor the festival by providing an outdoor space or some money. Or a local group of artists wants to sponsor the festival and provide some help with organizing. One or two lone festival organizers will have an easier time and create a more exciting event if they can connect with people or organizations in the community that offer a big name and some help.

Talking to possible customers is an important part of selling your art at a fair or festival.

- Plan. Planning for a festival can be complicated and has many steps. If you've ever thrown a birthday party, you'll know just how many different things you have to think about before the event. Now imagine planning for a festival, which is many times bigger and involves hundreds or thousands of people.

    Planning tasks include figuring out the space where the event will be held, as well as space for parking; picking a day (or days) and times; getting artists to sign up for booths to sell their art; finding bands and other entertainers; deciding on children's activities; figuring out what food will be served, if any; and decorating and putting up signs.

- Do outreach and promotion. If no one knows about an art festival, no one will show up! Festival organizers should spend some time advertising the event and reaching out to the community for attendees. Flyers, newspaper announcements, social media invites, and radio broadcasts can all spread the word. Organizers should add their festival to all local events calendars. Giving out ads to lots of local businesses to put up in their windows is a good idea. The more people are reminded of the festival, the more likely they are to come.

- Find volunteers. As the event gets closer, the organizer needs to find volunteers for the day of the festival. One person can't be everywhere, and volunteers are a great way to make the festival run more smoothly. Volunteers are useful for directing parking, selling and taking tickets, providing refreshments, setting up artists' tents and displays, and cleaning everything up at the end of the day. Volunteers may be rewarded with free admission or a thank-you present from the organizers.

SELLING AT A GALLERY

Artists have to work hard to get their art hung in galleries. If an artist doesn't have the money or the desire to start his own personal gallery,

Artists at this annual outdoor art fair in Evanston, Illinois, must bring their own tents or awnings. If a strong wind should blow through, it could be disastrous!

he'll have to look for an established gallery that is willing to display his pieces.

It isn't as simple as walking into a gallery and asking for space. Galleries are looking for artists who are easy to work with, talented, hard working, and have a bigger vision for their careers. Gallery owners will choose to show artists they think will sell, but also artists they think have something interesting to say.

Artists show galleries their work in the form of a portfolio. Portfolios are collections of an artist's work. Artists use them to show others just what they do, to try to convince them to display or buy some of their work. What a portfolio looks like exactly depends on the kind of art inside. A photographer would include several of her prints from the last few years. A painter would include prints of paintings, while a sculptor would include pictures of the actual works. In today's electronic world, more and more portfolios are online.

Artists hoping to show at a gallery should call ahead and make an appointment. Some artists just send their portfolio in, which may get ignored. Even worse, they may walk in unannounced and interrupt the gallery owner's day. The best thing to do is to get a referral from an artist the gallery already knows. That way, the people who work at the gallery are looking forward to meeting the new artist and have positive expectations.

Galleries then work with artists to choose which pieces to show and how much to price them for. The gallery owners offer valuable experience for artists who may just be starting out or who may not know that gallery's customers very well.

STARTING A GALLERY

You may not be ready yet to start your own gallery, but someday you might want to! Starting a gallery is a big business venture, and the people who do it are well prepared.

First, someone trying to open a gallery needs some funding. She

Some galleries may include both paintings and sculptures.

Make Connections: Art Dealers

One more way to make money through art is to become a dealer. The dealer links artists and art collectors by buying art and selling to customers he thinks would like those pieces. The dealer tries to buy art at a lower price than he sells it for, making money in the process by keeping a portion of each purchase.

might already have enough money to rent a space and set it up, but chances are she'll need money from somewhere else. Opening a gallery can be expensive! She may take out a loan from the bank, receive a **grant** from a local or national arts foundation, collect money from friends and family, or start an online donation campaign through a website like Kickstarter.

The owner will need to find a location and decide on the goals for the gallery as well. Will it be a space to display the owner's own work? Or will it highlight new artists, woman artists, nature artists, or someone else? Giving a gallery a purpose and theme will help it stand out from the crowd.

Once the gallery is funded and the owner has found a place to rent or buy, he needs to get it all set up and decorated. He may have to do some renovations or add extra walls, counters, and other features. That process can take several weeks to several months. At some point, the owner will also need to hire any employees he needs to help him run the gallery.

Marketing and advertising is important too, especially when a gallery is brand new. Flyers, Facebook, newspaper ads, radio ads, and

Deciding how to arrange lots of pieces of art can be a lot of work.

Make Connections: Similar Jobs

The U.S. Bureau of Labor Statistics has come up with a list of jobs that are similar to artists. People who like to paint may also be interested in becoming a museum curator, an art director at a newspaper or movie studio, a fashion designer, a graphic designer, an animator, or industrial designer. You can add gallery owner and festival organizer to this list.

word of mouth are all great ways to let people know a new gallery is opening, and to introduce them to what it's all about. With luck and some business sense and artistic talent, once the gallery is open it will attract lots of customers and become a successful establishment.

Research Project

Look for a few art festivals that are happening in your area. Try and find at least three—you can search for festivals that are farther away if you can't find that many in your region. Go to their websites, if they have them, and research what it would take to sell at each festival. Write down whether you would need to pay a fee or fill out an application. See if there are any restrictions for entry based on skill or type of art. Then compare each of the festivals. Which seem easiest to sell at? Which seem like they would give you the most business? Why?

Not all artists will be able to make a living selling their art at galleries or fairs. Having many ways to make money as an artist is the best way to make a living with your art.

MAKING A LIVING

Making a living through art can be tough. Very few people manage to make enough money for a comfortable life solely through art, and even fewer get rich.

The U.S Bureau of Labor Statistics says that the average artist made $44,380 per year in 2012. The lowest 10 percent earned $19,200,

Text-Dependent Questions

1. What do artists need to do before they can sell at an art festival?
2. Why do art festivals require artists to apply before they can have a booth?
3. Why should an art festival organizer connect with the local community?
4. How should an artist go about trying to get his or her work shown in a gallery?
5. How might an artist raise money to open up his or her own gallery?

while the top 10 percent earned more than $93,220. There's a wide range in how much artists can earn per year, depending on how they sell, what kind of art they produce, and how long they've been in the business.

Many artists end up working at another job either full or part time. Some artists have other interests and have another full-time job, filling up their free time with making and selling art. Others get a part-time job in something related to art (or something completely different), and focus on making art during their spare time. Artists might also work in art supply stores, as graphic designers, as illustrators, as art gallery attendants, or any number of other things.

Words to Understand

mission: The goals of you or the company you're making.
accessible: Able to be reached or used.
templates: Designs that have already been made so you don't have to design your own.

Chapter Four

How Do I Get Involved in Art Festivals and Galleries?

Getting involved in art festivals or galleries might seem daunting. But if you can get some experience in as a young person, you'll be more ready to be a professional artist or even start your own festival or gallery someday. You can get involved on lots of different levels, from volunteering to selling your own art to organizing an event.

VOLUNTEER

If you're not ready to actually organize an art festival or gallery, volunteering is a great way to see how things work and to get some experience.

Volunteering to do face painting could be a great way to get involved with an art festival while using some of your artistic skills.

Art festivals always need lots and lots of volunteers. Look up when festivals happen near you, and see if there's a contact e-mail or phone number you should use to get in touch with the organizers. You might even find a direct link to a volunteer signup right on a website.

As a volunteer, you could be asked to do any number of things. You might help artists set up their booths or set up tables and chairs for the eating area. You might stand at the festival entrance and take tickets or tell festival-goers where to walk.

If you want to volunteer behind the scenes and get involved in the planning, let the organizers know. They might be able to find you a job contacting sponsors, getting donations for a raffle, or planning entertainment. The more experience you have with festivals, the more responsibility you'll get, especially if you can prove you're responsible and willing to work hard.

You might also be able to find ways to volunteer at an art gallery. Search around for the galleries near you. A good bet is to volunteer for special events they're hosting, such as gallery openings or public showcases. Special events require more work than is ordinarily needed, and gallery owners and curators may be looking for some extra help.

Art galleries might need volunteers to do everyday tasks too. You could end up filing papers, or sitting at the desk during open hours to answer people's first questions. You never know until you ask—so call up a gallery or visit one to find out if it could use your help.

SELL YOUR STUFF

If you're a beginning artist and you want to start selling your art, festivals are a great place to start. You can buy a spot at several festivals in your area, and hopefully start making back enough money to at least fund your artistic talent.

Some artists actually create small pieces of art while they're at a festival. This could be a great opportunity for you to ask questions and learn more.

Before you even start selling, you should consider going to some festivals to see what they're like. Take a look at the booths artists have set up. What do they look like? What kinds of art are being sold? How many booths are at each festival? Make sure selling at a festival is something you really want to do.

You need some business skills if you're going to venture into selling art at festivals. Starting to sell at a festival requires some money up front, so you'll need to create a budget and see how much money you'll need. To sell at festivals, you need to buy a tent, a table and chairs, and display equipment. Artists also usually have to pay a fee to sell at each festival they attend.

Then you'll need to figure out what sells so that you're not just sitting at your table all day watching customers pass by you. You can try to sell a few more expensive things, especially if you think a festival will attract customers who are willing to spend some money. You'll also want to sell some less expensive pieces, so that customers without a lot of money can still buy something from you. For example, if you sell paintings, you might consider offering cheaper prints and cards of those paintings. You'll figure out how much people are willing to pay for your art over time. You can check out the prices of other artists' work to get a sense of what you should charge for your own. If lots of people are buying from you, try raising your prices a little to see if as many people are still willing to buy. And if no one seems to be buying your art, lower your prices!

You can even offer sales from time to time, especially if you want to clear out old art to make room for new stuff you're making. Buy-one-get-one-free or including free note cards with a purchase may convince more customers to make purchases than would otherwise. Some artists are willing to bargain with customers too, but that's up to you.

A business plan has certain elements that will help you get organized and plan for the future.

Make Connections: Supplies

Artists who sell at festivals need a lot of equipment. Among other things, they need:

- a folding tent or awning
- weights to keep the tent on the ground
- chair and tables
- grid wall for hanging art
- print racks or other display cases
- price tags
- decorations such as tablecloths
- clamps for securing tablecloths
- business cards
- extra cash and change
- calculator
- lighting if showing at night

CREATING A BUSINESS PLAN

No matter if you're selling art an art festival, organizing your own festival, or opening an art gallery, you're starting a business. To make things even smoother, you could create a business plan. People who are just starting businesses often find that creating a business plan gives them a head start. A business plan is like a roadmap that tells you where you're going so you're in for fewer surprises.

When you have big goals for the future, it's best to break them down into smaller goals. These goals can then serve as your roadmap. As you achieve each one, you know what to do next.

A business plan has several sections that lay out everything you—or someone reading about your business—needs to know. First, write out a business summary. What is your business called? What do you sell? Include a brief history of how you started your business. This section shouldn't be more than a paragraph or two.

Next, write down a **mission** statement. In one or two sentences, what do you hope to achieve with your business? Why specifically are you selling art? Your mission statement should include more than just making a lot of money. Maybe you want to make art more **accessible** to young people, or you want to donate a portion of your profits to arts education. Along with your mission statement, write down a list of goals over the short and long term. Selling at five art festivals next year or creating and pricing ten new paintings over the next six months are examples of some business goals.

After that, a business plan should include how your business is organized. As an artist, you may not have anyone helping you with your business, but if you have employees you should write about them. Otherwise, describe how you organize the time you devote to your business. Also include if you have any goals for hiring someone in the future.

Business plans often have a market analysis next. What does the art industry look like for your particular medium and specialty? What sorts of changes is it going through and how does that affect you?

Conduct a SWOT analysis. SWOT stands for Strengths, Weaknesses, Opportunities, and Threats. Your business already has strengths and weaknesses. And you can take advantage of opportunities and keep threats in mind in order to be successful. An opportunity might be that there are few artists of your sort in your town, so you have the chance to get a lot of customers. A threat might be that the supplies you need for your art are becoming more and more expensive.

Business plans also include financial plans, which focus on the money side of the business. This is where your budget comes in, along with the prices you'll set for your art. How much do you have to pay to make and sell your art? And where are you going to get that money? How much do you anticipate your business making? Your ultimate goal should be to make more than you're paying.

You can always change your business plan as you go along; plans aren't set in stone. Use your plan as a way to keep moving forward and anticipate any challenges—and successes—you'll have. Your business will thank you for it!

YOUR OWN GALLERY SHOWS

At this point in your career, you're probably still working on improving your art. But if you feel like it's ready for display and sale in a gallery, go for it! Your best bet may be to look for galleries that are having shows of young people's art. You could also try asking around at local cafés and other businesses that have art displayed on their walls. Local businesses are usually a little more low key than formal art galleries, and they may be happy to help launch your art career.

Even if you don't have your art in a physical gallery, you can set up an online gallery pretty easily. You can potentially reach far more people online than you can through a physical store.

Making your website isn't hard. You can create your own website from *templates* online, at sites like Foliotwist, which cost money. Some website platforms are free, such as Wix, Weebly, and Squarespace. Other places to check out include ArtPal, Craigslist, and Fine Art America. You might also decide to have a bigger social media presence online by setting up a Facebook and Twitter account for your art business.

An online gallery should obviously have pictures of all your art. It should also have news and events, such as upcoming art shows where you'll be selling. Be sure to include your contact information and maybe even an ordering form so customers can make purchases from you directly on the website. (Using PayPal is a good way to be able to take payments.) Also include information about yourself as the artist, so customers can get to know you a little.

You could also set up your own art store online at a place like Etsy.com. You create a virtual store that is grouped together with thousands of other stores. When someone is looking for a piece of handmade jewelry, for example, she'll visit Etsy and search for the kind of jewelry she wants. If what she wants matches what you're selling, your store will pop up and she can explore all the pieces you have online.

NETWORKING

Networking is a great skill to have, no matter your profession. Networking involves connecting with lots and lots of people who can help you get ahead in your career, while you can help them too. You might meet with people who are already established artists, festival organizers, or gallery owners. They can give you advice, and may even offer to mentor you or steer you toward jobs. People can tell you which festivals would be best for you, which galleries to approach, and how to start your own business. Always be open to new acquaintances, since you never know how you can help each other out.

Make time to do some networking, even if you're shy. Talk to artists at art festivals about how they got there. Visit gallery opening receptions and see if anyone is willing to give a young businessperson some advice and encouragement. See if your art teachers can give you the contact information for people who can help you. People in the art world will get to know who you are if you meet them enough times.

KEEP MAKING ART

Even with all of these business ventures, don't forget your art. Keep practicing and producing more art for sale. Over time, you'll develop an

Research Project

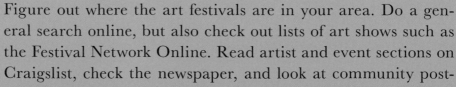

Figure out where the art festivals are in your area. Do a general search online, but also check out lists of art shows such as the Festival Network Online. Read artist and event sections on Craigslist, check the newspaper, and look at community posting boards. Write down a list of all the art festivals you could sell at. Even if you're not interested in selling art right now, go check them out since they're a great gathering space for art and artists of all kinds!

even more distinctive style and gain more customers who want to buy your work.

Take classes at school if you can. Try out some new types of art, which might inspire you. If you're normally a photographer, take a painting class. You might learn more about how to compose a picture through the class, or decide on a new subject to photograph.

You can also look for classes at local community education centers and museums. Many places offer classes like pottery, jewelry making, watercolor, and more. You might find more variety than at school.

If you can't find any classes to take, just make art at home! Even if you are taking a class, creating art is something that can happen whenever you feel inspired. Get a few supplies and find a space where you feel comfortable making art. Then practice! Try out new things. If you're selling your art, your customers may get excited when you introduce new forms of art and new styles, so play around and see what sells.

Text-Dependent Questions

1. Where could you volunteer to get some more experience selling art at festivals or galleries?
2. How should you set prices for the art you're trying to sell?
3. What is a business plan and why is it useful for people just starting out with selling art?
4. Name the parts of a business plan.
5. What are some ways to set up an online art gallery?

If you're an artist or interested in art, though, you should definitely consider getting involved in art festivals and art galleries. They can take your interest to the next level, turning art into a career. Whether you're sitting at a festival booth selling handmade jewelry or setting up a gallery of your paintings online, you'll be gaining more in depth experience while you enter the world of art as business.

Find Out More

Online

100 Greatest Sculptures Ever
www.visual-arts-cork.com/greatest-sculptures-ever.htm

Biography.com: Famous Sculptors
www.biography.com/people/groups/sculptors

International Sculpture Center
www.sculpture.org

Sculptor.org
www.sculptor.org

U.S. Bureau of Labor Statistics: Fine Artists
www.bls.gov/oes/current/oes271013.htm

In Books

Brown, Claire Waite. *The Sculpting Techniques Bible: An Essential Illustrated Reference for Both Beginner and Experienced Sculptors*. Edison, N.J.: Chartwell Books, 2006.

Emert, Phyllis. *Pottery (Eye on Art)*. Farmington Hills, Mich.: Lucent Books, 2008.

Mariotti, Steve. *The Young Entrepreneur's Guide to Starting and Running a Business*. New York: Times Books, 2012.

McNeese, Tim. *Michelangelo: Painter, Sculptor, and Architect*. New York: Chelsea House Publishing, 2005.

Nardo, Don. *Sculpture (Eye on Art)*. Farmington Hills, Mich.: Lucent Books, 2006.

Series Glossary of Key Terms

Abstract: Made up of shapes that are symbolic. You might not be able to tell what a piece of abstract art is just by looking at it.

Classical: A certain kind of art traditional to the ancient Greek and Roman civilizations. In music, it refers to music in a European tradition that includes opera and symphony and that is generally considered more serious than other kinds of music.

Culture: All the arts, social meanings, thoughts, and behaviors that are common in a certain country or group.

Gallery: A room or a building that displays art.

Genre: A category of art, all with similar characteristics or styles.

Impressionism: A style of painting that focuses more on the artist's perception of movement and lighting than what something actually looks like.

Improvisation: Created without planning or preparation.

Medium (media): The materials or techniques used to create a work of art. Oil paints are a medium. So is digital photography.

Pitch: How high or low a musical note is; where it falls on a scale.

Portfolio: A collection of some of the art an artist has created, to show off her talents.

Realism: Art that tries to show something exactly as it appears in real life.

Renaissance: A period of rapid artistic and literary development during the 1500s–1700s, or the name of the artistic style from this period.

Studio: A place where an artist can work and create his art.

Style: A certain way of creating art specific to a person or time period.

Technique: A certain way of creating a piece of art.

Tempo: How fast a piece of music goes.

Venue: The location or facility where an event takes place.

Index

About the Author

Z.B. Hill is a an author and publicist living in Binghamton, New York. He has a special interest in education and how art can be used in the classroom.

Picture Credits

Dreamstime.com:
6: Anthony Aneese Totah Jr
8: Dimaberkut
12: Pavel Losevsky , Wiktor Wojtas
14: Chi Wai Li
18: Vadim Kulikov
28: Smontgom65
30: Wendy Leber
32: Ajay Bhaskar
34: Smontgom65
36: Nathan Resnick
38: Gabrielnyta
40: Desertofsnowflake
42: Ekaterina Bykova

44: Ajay Bhaskar
46: Pavel Losevsky
48: Dimaberkut

Fotolia.com:
10: shotsstudio
20: Vladislav Gajic
22: gianliguori
23: anghifoto
24: Lorraine Swanson
50: Minerva Studio
52: style67

26: Michael F. James